PARASITES

Tapeworms

Toney Allman

KIDHAVEN
PRESS™

THOMSON
★
GALE™

San Diego • Detroit • New York • San Francisco • Cleveland
New Haven, Conn. • Waterville, Maine • London • Munich

THOMSON

™

GALE

For more information, contact
KidHaven Press
27500 Drake Rd.
Farmington Hills, MI 48331-3535
Or you can visit our Internet site at http://www.gale.com

LIBRARY OF CONGRESS CATALOGING-IN-PUBLICATION DATA

Allman, Toney.
  Tapeworms / Toney Allman.
    v. cm. — (Parasites)
Includes bibliographical references (p.   ).
Contents: Giant parasites—Tapeworm invasion—Tapeworm tales—Breaking the tapeworm life cycle.
  ISBN 0-7377-1783-1
1. Tapeworm infections—Juvenile literature. 2. Tapeworms—Juvenile literature. [Tapeworms.] I. Title. II. Series.
  RC184.T5A45 2004
  616.9'64—dc21

                                                                2004003945

Printed in China

CONTENTS

Giant Parasites

Tapeworms are strange and ugly creatures that grow and live inside other animals. Tapeworms are worms, but they do not live or act like other worms. Tapeworms are **parasites**. A parasite is an animal that lives and feeds off another living animal or person. That animal or person is called a **host**. Like all parasites, tapeworms cannot live on their own. The human tapeworm lives its life inside the body of a person, in the **intestine**. Without this host's body for a home, the tapeworm is helpless. It cannot search for food or take

Opposite: Tapeworms live and grow in the intestines of people and animals.

care of itself. It has no legs, no bones, no teeth or claws. It has no eyes or ears. It cannot eat food by itself because it has no mouth, no stomach, and no intestines for digesting food. It does not even have a real head! Still, when a tapeworm has a person to live in, it gets along very well with what it does have.

The Tapeworm Body

Instead of a head, the tapeworm has a **scolex**. The scolex looks like a head, but it is made up of hooks and suckers that the tapeworm uses to cling to the host's intestine. The tapeworm also has a neck. It is from the neck that the tapeworm's body parts grow. The rest of the tapeworm's body is just a long chain of **segments** which make tapeworm eggs. These segments are like the beads in a necklace, all strung together, except that they are flat and narrow. So the tapeworm's body is like a long, soft, segmented ribbon with a scolex on top. All along this ribbon are little feathery "fingers" that can mesh with the host's intestinal wall and absorb food for the tapeworm.

When the tapeworm begins its life in a person's intestine, it is very small. It is only about one-quarter inch long. Its body is just a scolex and a neck. The scolex attaches to the intestine with its suckers and hooks. Now the tapeworm has a place to live and grow. All it has to do is stay put in its body home.

Home Sweet Home

The host's intestine is a sloshing ocean of half-digested food. The muscles of the intestine constantly ripple and pulse, creating a flowing, rocking

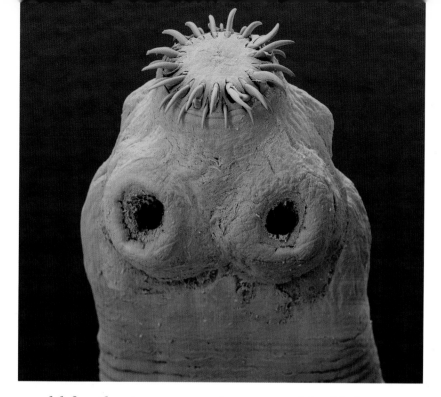

world for the tapeworm to cope with. If the tapeworm is not careful, it can be pushed out of its home altogether. Yet, it does cope. It thrives. The tapeworm clings tightly with its suckers and hooks. It interlocks with the intestinal wall using its tiny "fingers." When the host eats and digests food, the tapeworm soaks up some of the food into its own body. It does not need a stomach or

An Efficient Parasite

1 Four large suckers and hooked teeth help the tapeworm cling to the host's intestine.

2 Body segments grow from the neck area. Each body segment produces many eggs.

3 Ribbon-like segments absorb digested food from the host's intestine.

intestines of its own. The food is already digested for it by the host.

As the tapeworm takes in its food, it grows by adding segments to its body. The little "fingers" on these new segments soak up more food. After only three or four months, the tapeworm can be five feet long with hundreds of segments. If the tapeworm lives for many years, it can sometimes grow to be sixty feet long with thousands of segments. That is as long as an eighteen-wheel truck! It never stops growing as long as it is alive, and a tapeworm can live for thirty years.

The Uninvited Guest

During all those years, the human host is feeding the uninvited tapeworm guest. Quietly, the hidden tapeworm steals more and more food. Secretly, the tapeworm grows bigger. Yet, often, the person does not know that there is an invader inside or how the thief came to be there.

Tapeworm Invasion

People get tapeworms from the food they eat. Before becoming adults, young tapeworms have to live in another animal that will be eaten by a person. This in-between animal is called the tapeworm's **intermediate host**. For human tapeworms, these animals are usually cows, pigs, or fish.

Eggs

Each segment in the mature tapeworm's body is a little egg factory. The tapeworm does not need a mate to make eggs. Its segments have both male and female parts to make living eggs. When the eggs are ready in a segment, the segment breaks off the end of the tapeworm. It travels through the host's body and is passed out in the person's **feces**. The eggs in

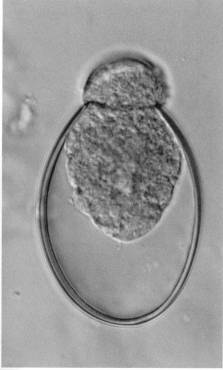

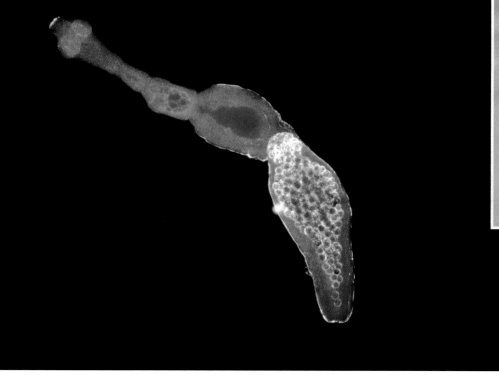

The end segment of a tapeworm's body breaks off (left) after it has become filled with eggs (above).

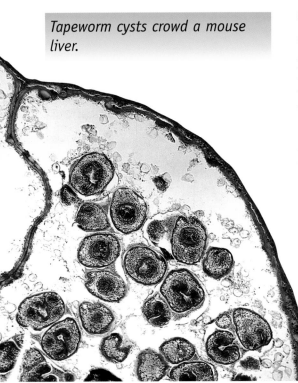

Tapeworm cysts crowd a mouse liver.

this segment are so tiny they can only be seen with a microscope, and there are thousands of them.

In places where there is no modern plumbing, people's waste ends up in rivers or fields or ditches. The feces and eggs lie outdoors and are exposed to the rain and sun. They are stepped in and carried around on feet. The eggs must now find an intermediate host to hatch in. Some pork tapeworm eggs are formed and eaten by pigs. Some beef tapeworm eggs land on green grass and are eaten by cows. Some fish tapeworm eggs fall in water and are eaten by tiny crustaceans that are eaten by fish. These eggs all hatch in the right kind of home. **Larvae** are born.

Cysts

A larva is a tapeworm child, but it does not look like a tapeworm. Under a microscope, it looks a bit like a leaf. The larva hatches in the intermediate host's intestine. It bores through the intestinal wall using an **enzyme**. It rides along the bloodstream until it gets to a muscle. Here it stops and forms a **cyst**, a hard shell, around itself. The cyst is

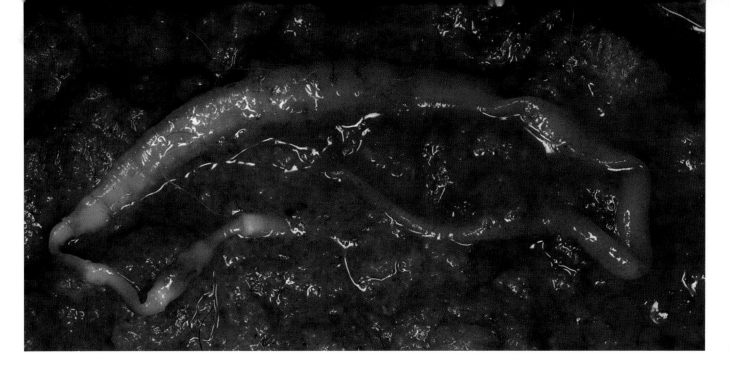

about the size and shape of a small marble or shiny white pearl. Inside this cyst, the larva transforms into a scolex. The cyst waits in the intermediate host's muscle. It can wait for years.

When a cow or pig intermediate host is butchered, the muscles become a steak or a roast or a pork chop. When a fish intermediate host is caught, it may become sashimi or a fish cake. If any of this meat is not well cooked, a person eats

Tapeworms depend on their hosts for survival. Here, segments of a tapeworm appear in a dog's vomit.

 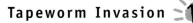

Tapeworms can grow thousands of segments and reach up to sixty feet in length.

living cysts along with the food. Any cyst swallowed into the intestine breaks open. Out comes the scolex. It attaches to the person's intestinal wall and starts growing segments. The tapeworm **life cycle** starts all over again.

CHAPTER 3

Tapeworm Tales

Until 1854, people did not know about the tapeworm life cycle. They believed that tapeworms appeared by magic in the body. They also ate a lot of meat that had shiny white pearls or shells inside. In Germany, a doctor named Friedrich Küchenmeister thought maybe these pearly shells were where tapeworms came from.

15

A Gory Test

Dr. Küchenmeister thought up an experiment to prove his idea. He pulled shells from some pork and stirred them into a noodle soup. He took his soup to a prison and offered it to a murderer who was about to be executed. The prisoner ate two bowls full. Three days later, the prisoner had his head cut off. Dr. Küchenmeister got the murderer's

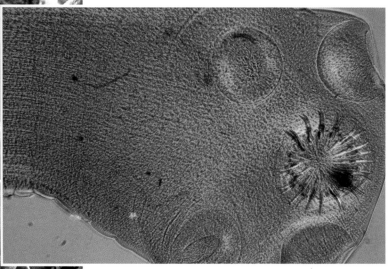

German doctor Friedrich Küchenmeister discovered tapeworms (above) growing in the intestine (left) of a prisoner in 1854.

body and cut it open. Inside the intestine, he found small tapeworms already attached and growing. Dr. Küchenmeister's shells were really tapeworm cysts in their intermediate host. Now people understood that tapeworms came from cysts in the food they ate.

When the Life Cycle Goes Wrong

Pork tapeworms are especially dangerous to people, not because of eating cysts and growing tapeworms, but because people can become accidental intermediate hosts for cysts. Pork tapeworm eggs in a person's feces can get on hands during bathroom use and then be swallowed or passed on to other people. These eggs hatch in a person instead of a pig. The larvae can travel anywhere in the person's body but often end up in the brain or eyes. They settle down to make cysts, but a human brain is not the same as a pig's muscle. The cyst is in the wrong intermediate host. It becomes sick and swells up with fluid. It will die, but its dying puts the person in terrible danger.

A person with a swelling cyst in the brain is horribly sick. As the cyst swells, it pushes on brain tissue, causing holes in the brain. Sometimes the cyst swells so much that it explodes. A cyst can grow as big as an orange and then explode with such force that the person's skull is fractured. **Seizures**, brain damage, and death are the results of cyst invasion of the brain. Around the world, fifty thousand people every year die from tapeworm cysts.

Kill a Tapeworm, Not!

Because of the trouble tapeworms and their cysts can cause, frightened people have thought up many stories about how to kill them. One **myth** is that a tapeworm can be tricked into crawling out of a person's mouth. People who believe this starve themselves for a week. Then they hold a bowl of soup to their lips. They believe the starving tapeworm will smell the soup and crawl up to the mouth where they can pull it out. This is impossible.

Tapeworms cannot crawl through the body and have no noses with which to smell.

Another story is that tapeworms can be poisoned by certain foods that people eat. The myth

Tapeworm cysts, like these from a human lung, are extremely dangerous and can even cause death.

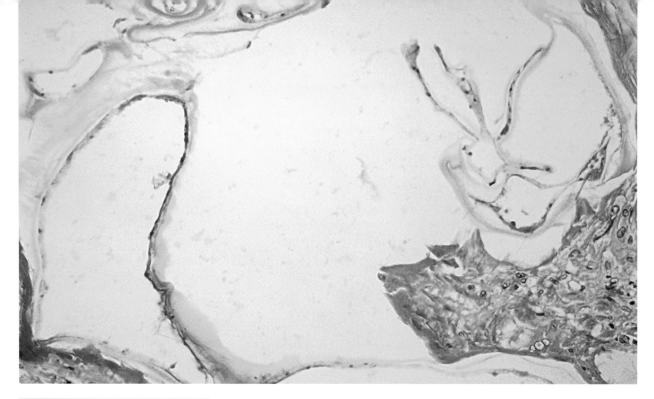

This liver is infected with tapeworm cysts.

is that onions, garlic, pumpkin seeds, and whiskey taste so bad to the tapeworm that it lets go of the intestine and dies or leaves the body. Tapeworms cannot taste, though, and are not poisoned by any special food.

People, however, are not helpless hosts. Tapeworm invasions can be fought if the tapeworm life cycle is understood.

CHAPTER 4

Breaking the Tapeworm Life Cycle

If tapeworm eggs cannot hatch, no new cysts can form. If living cysts are not eaten by people, no human tapeworms can grow. If a tapeworm is destroyed, its life as an egg factory is ended. A successful attack on the life cycle at any point prevents tapeworm invasion.

Ready, Set, Flush

A tapeworm's greatest enemy is a toilet! When people flush toilets, the waste is carried into sewers and then to sewage treatment plants. There, wastes are cleaned and purified before any water or solids are sent back into rivers or to the earth. People break the tapeworm life cycle by flushing eggs away.

Tapeworm invasions are common in poor countries (opposite) where sewage and other wastes are dumped directly into rivers (right).

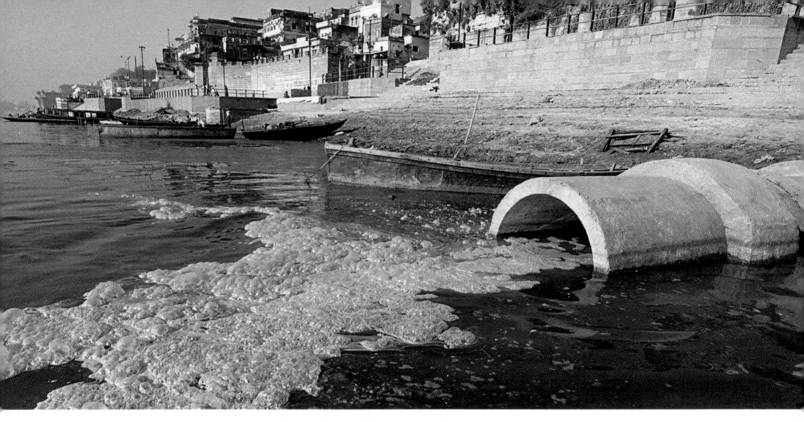

Most tapeworm invasions happen in poor countries where people do not have toilets. They use outhouses or even ditches. Or their cities do not have sewage treatment plants to clean the sewage. It just gets dumped in a river. If people or animals drink the river water, they swallow eggs. Without toilets and water faucets, it is hard to be clean.

And Use the Water Faucet

Cleanliness kills tapeworm eggs. People who wash their hands after bathroom use wash away tapeworm eggs. No eggs can be swallowed or passed on to other people. People who never drink water from a river or stream cannot swallow tapeworm eggs accidentally. Clean water for washing and drinking prevents tapeworm invasion.

Cysts: Cook It or Avoid It!

The tapeworm life cycle can also be broken by destroying cysts. In modern countries, governments have rules about the safety of meat. Meat is inspected, and meat with cysts inside cannot be sold. People in these countries are quite safe from tapeworm invasion. However, even people who are not this lucky can be safe. Cysts are killed by heat. When meat is cooked well done, any cysts in it are killed. Eating a dead cyst can do no harm.

Some people enjoy eating raw fish dishes like sushi or sashimi. Fish tapeworm cysts can be hiding in this meat. As sashimi and sushi have become popular around the world, fish tape-worms have become common. Only cooked fish is safe.

Avoiding meat that might be infected also keeps people safe. In Muslim countries, people do not eat pork because it is forbidden by the **Koran**. These

Doctors removed this full-grown tapeworm from an eighteen-month-old child.

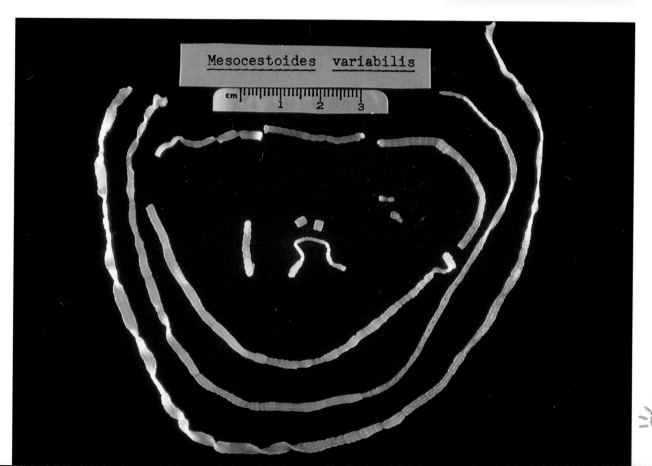

people do not get pork tapeworms or pork cyst sicknesses. Never eating live cysts breaks the tapeworm life cycle and prevents tapeworm invasions.

Tapeworms: Doctor, Help!

If prevention fails, the tapeworm itself must be killed. When a person has a tapeworm growing inside, a doctor prescribes a medicine so strong

Jars containing human tapeworms are displayed at a museum.

that it poisons the tapeworm. Usually, the person has to swallow only one dose of medicine to kill the tapeworm. Cysts can also be killed with medicine or surgery.

Tapeworms will never be wiped out completely because tapeworms live in every kind of animal, not just people. Still, people can someday make tapeworms rare by being clean and careful. Knowledge of the tapeworm life cycle is the most important weapon in the fight against these parasites.

cyst: A pearly shell in the intermediate host's muscle. It is the middle stage in the tapeworm life cycle.

enzyme: A protein made by the tapeworm larva to chemically eat through the intestinal wall.

feces: Bowel movements or wastes that are passed out of the body.

host: The animal or person in which a parasite lives.

intermediate host: The in-between animal in which tapeworm cysts must live before they can grow into tapeworms.

intestine: The coiled tube part of the digestive system, below the stomach. In the intestines, digestion is finished and food absorbed, and then wastes are passed out of the body.

Koran: The sacred book of Islam.

larva, larvae: The newly hatched, earliest stage of tapeworm growth. Larvae is plural.

life cycle: The different stages of development a tapeworm goes through, from egg to larva to cyst to mature animal to producing eggs again.

myth: A popular story, legend, or belief that is not based in fact.

parasite: An animal that feeds on or grows in another animal without giving anything in return.

scolex: Headlike part of the tapeworm that holds fast to the intestine with suckers and hooks.

segment: Any one of the hundreds of sections or parts of the tapeworm's body that makes eggs.

seizure: A sudden attack of brain malfunction causing loss of consciousness, loss of muscle control, or confusion.

Book

Brian Ward, *Epidemic.* New York: Dorling Kindersley, 2000. This book describes many different types of parasites and diseases.

Websites

Welcome to Worm Learn (http://home.austernet.com). This website is for high school students, but clicking the different images will show interesting pictures of human and animal tapeworms and other parasites.

The Yuckiest Site on the Internet (http://yucky.kids. discovery.com). Visit Wendell Worm and read his interview with his cousin, Tommi Tapeworm.

INDEX

ABOUT THE AUTHOR

Toney Allman holds degrees from Ohio State University and the University of Hawaii. She now lives in Virginia, where she enjoys reading, gardening, and exploring the woods with her Saint Bernard. So far, they have found plenty of birds and squirrels but very few parasites.